LET'S EXPLORE SCIENCE

CELLS

AUTHOR
SUSAN MARKOWITZ
MEREDITH

ROURKE PUBLISHING

Vero Beach, Florida 32964

www.rourkepublishing.com

PHOTO CREDITS: © Bruce Rolff: Title Page; © Janne Ahvo: 3; © Svetlana Larina: 4; © Lisa Thornberg: 4; © poco_bw: 4; © Sebastian Kaulitzki: 5, 7, 14, 16, 32, 35; © 21 TORR archives Gmbtt: 5; © Bogden Pop: 7; © Karl Dolenc: 7; © ChristianAnthony: 7; © Wikipedia: 7, 40, 41; © Molecular Expressions: 7; © roccomontoya: 9; © Jacob Wackerhausen: 10; © jangeltun: 11; © Alexonline: 12; © Diane Labombarbe: 13; © nicolesy: 17; ©Stefan Kline: 21; © RTimages: 21; © Jason Register: 22, 23, 33, 37; © Kiyoshi Takahase Segundo: 24; © Henrik Jonsson: 25, 32, 38; © james steidl: 27; © iLexx: 28; © Olga Bogatyrenko: 31; © digitalskillet: 34; © Monika Wisniewska: 39; © Sven Hoppe: 43; © Jayson Punwani: 43; © Laurence Gough: 44, 45

Edited by Kelli L. Hicks

Cover and Interior design by Teri Intzegian

Library of Congress Cataloging-in-Publication Data

Meredith, Susan, 1951-
 Cells / Susan Meredith.
   p. cm. -- (Let's explore science)
 Includes index.
 ISBN 978-1-60694-412-7 (hard cover)
 ISBN 978-1-60694-530-8 (soft cover)
 1. Cells--Juvenile literature. I. Title.
 QH582.5.M47 2010
 571.6--dc22

                                2009005740

Printed in the USA

CG/CG

ROURKE PUBLISHING

www.rourkepublishing.com - rourke@rourkepublishing.com
Post Office Box 643328 Vero Beach, Florida 32964

Table of Contents

CHAPTER ONE

Units of Life

All living things have something basic in common: **cells**. Most organisms consist of only one cell. The rest of us, from humans to fleas to flowers, are multi-celled.

Whatever the organism, its cells are usually very small. A typical cell is about 1/1,000 of an inch (0.0025 centimeters) in diameter. It takes a microscope to see them. Added together, the cells in a human total more than 10 trillion. Whales have even more cells. The larger the organism, the more cells it contains.

DID YOU KNOW?

Some single-celled organisms called **bacteria** are so tiny that five side-by-side measure only 1/10,000 of an inch (0.00025 centimeters).

One amazing cell that you can see without magnification is an egg. Eggs, such as this enormous ostrich egg, are a single cell that when fertilized divides many times and develops into a chick.

Many Shapes

Cells may be small, but they don't all look alike. They have many different shapes. Single-celled plants called algae, for example, often look like balls. But a type of algae known as a diatom may have the shape of a rod, cube, star, or pyramid. Single-celled animals have even more shapes.

The cells of multicellular organisms usually differ from one another in shape, and in function. Human muscle cells, for instance, are long and thin while red blood cells are disk-like. In general, animal cells have a greater variety of shapes than plant cells. Many of the cells inside plants look like boxes.

DID YOU KNOW?

Robert Hooke first used the term cell in 1665. Looking at a piece of cork under a microscope, he noticed its many boxlike shapes.

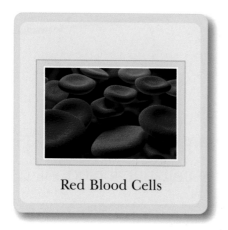

Red Blood Cells

Diatom

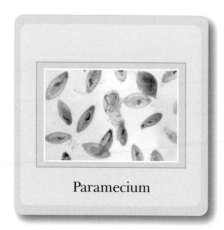

Paramecium

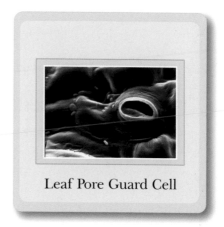

Leaf Pore Guard Cell

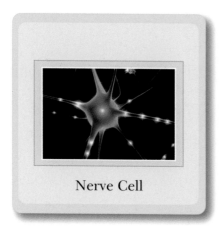

Nerve Cell

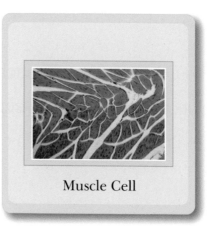

Muscle Cell

Inside the Cell

Whatever its size or shape, every cell is busy. Like a tiny factory, its different parts keep the cell functioning. All cells have the same basic parts: 1) a cell membrane, 2) cytoplasm, and 3) a control center.

The cell membrane is the cell's outer covering. It works like a filter that lets only certain substances in and out of the cell.

Cytoplasm is the colorless, jellylike matter inside the cell. It holds all the cell's various parts.

The control center of each cell directs all of its activities. In multicellular and many single-celled organisms, this center is an enclosed area called the **nucleus**.

The nucleus houses the cell's master plan. This plan is a set of instructions that each cell needs to work properly.

Typical Animal Cell

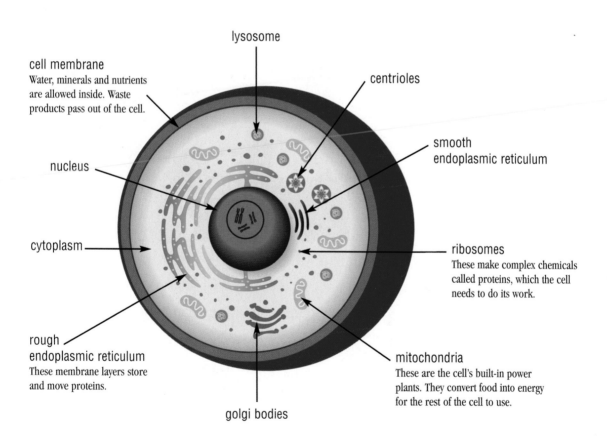

lysosome

centrioles

cell membrane
Water, minerals and nutrients are allowed inside. Waste products pass out of the cell.

smooth endoplasmic reticulum

nucleus

cytoplasm

ribosomes
These make complex chemicals called proteins, which the cell needs to do its work.

rough endoplasmic reticulum
These membrane layers store and move proteins.

mitochondria
These are the cell's built-in power plants. They convert food into energy for the rest of the cell to use.

golgi bodies

A Look at the Nucleus

Inside the nucleus, threadlike **chromosomes** carry the cell's instructions. A chromosome consists of many units called **genes**. Each gene contains a single instruction.

One or more genes may be responsible for such things as a person's eye or hair color. These qualities, or **traits**, make one organism different from another.

Every gene in a chromosome is made of a chemical material called DNA. The letters stand for Deoxyribonucleic Acid. The arrangement of the DNA in a gene (or group of genes) is important. One arrangement may produce brown hair. A different DNA arrangement would produce red hair.

The structure of DNA

Adenine

Thymine

Guanine

Cytosine

base pairs

sugar phosphate backbone

Human chromosomes carry tens of thousands of genes.

Plant Cells

Plant cells have the same basic parts as other cells. But a plant cell also has some special features. For one, a stiff outer wall surrounds its cell membrane. The cell wall gives extra protection to the cell.

Every plant cell also contains a large sac for fluid. It's called a **vacuole**. The fluid inside keeps the cell strong and sturdy.

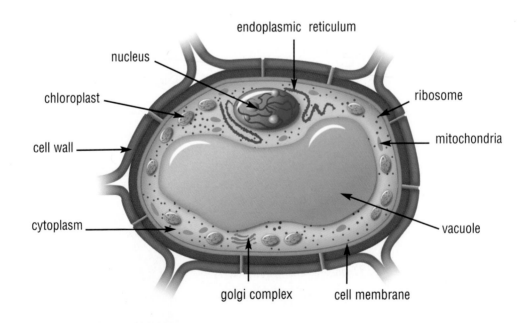

endoplasmic reticulum

nucleus

chloroplast

ribosome

cell wall

mitochondria

cytoplasm

vacuole

golgi complex

cell membrane

Food Factories

Plant cells are special in another way. Their leaf cells make their own food in a process called **photosynthesis**. The process happens inside the cell's chloroplasts. These small disks contain green matter called **chlorophyll**. During the day, the chlorophyll absorbs energy from the Sun's rays. The chloroplast uses the energy to combine carbon dioxide and water, which the cell brings in. This mixture forms a high-energy sugar. Plant cells use this food to do their work. As a by-product of photosynthesis, the cells give off oxygen.

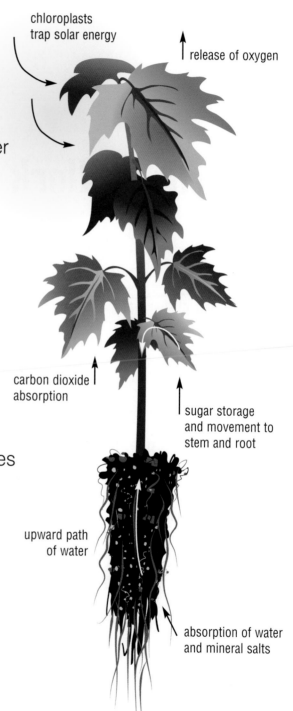

chloroplasts trap solar energy

release of oxygen

carbon dioxide absorption

sugar storage and movement to stem and root

upward path of water

absorption of water and mineral salts

CHAPTER TWO

Cells At Work

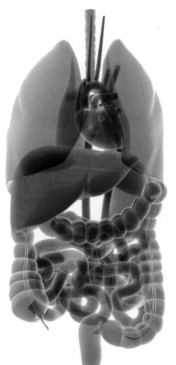

Humans have over 200 kinds of cells.

Every cell has work to do. But different cells may have different jobs. In multicellular organisms, cells with the same type of job often work together. These groups of specialized cells form tissue. In turn, tissues often group together to form larger units, called organs. The heart is an organ; so is the stomach.

The cells of each organ or tissue have specific jobs. In humans, for instance, different groups of muscle cells are in charge of walking, throwing, chewing food—even blinking.

Muscle Cells

In each muscle tissue, the cells work in bundles. An arm muscle, for example, is made of thousands of long, tube-like cells called muscle fibers. When the muscle moves, it tightens, or contracts. Each of its muscle cells contracts, too. Muscle cells have the right structure to contract easily.

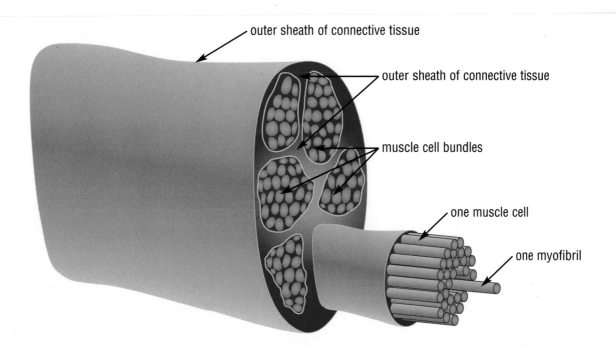

outer sheath of connective tissue

outer sheath of connective tissue

muscle cell bundles

one muscle cell

one myofibril

Nerve Cells

Sending messages is the job of nerve cells, or **neurons**. Cordlike bundles of neurons, called nerves, spread like branches through the body. All the branches combined form the nervous system. It consists of billions of nerve cells.

Messages move rapidly in the nervous system. This happens in a person who suddenly spots a fast-moving car on the street. Instantly, that person jumps back to the curb.

Some nerve messages, or impulses, travel at 300 feet (90 meters) per second.

DID YOU KNOW?

Flowers vary in the number and placement of their stamens. Sometimes stamens are small and hard to see. In other flowers, the stamens stand out, their tube-like anthers loaded with pollen.

Pistils differ among flower species. Some flowers contain one pistil; many have two or more. Whatever their differences, all flowers have the same purpose: reproduction. This white lily flower has both male and female flowers on the same plant, making it's job of reproduction easy.

CHAPTER FOUR

Cell Diseases

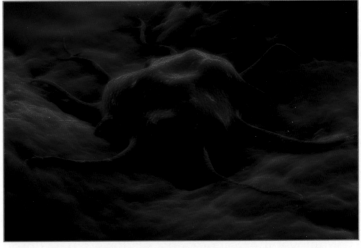

Usually cells function properly. They grow and repair themselves to do their work. They also divide in an orderly way. But things go wrong from time to time.

Cancer cells can break away from where they started and spread the cancer to other parts of the body.

Wild Cells

Sometimes certain cells in multicellular organisms cannot stop dividing. These wild cells, called cancer cells, cause problems. They get in the way of normal cells trying to function. Cancer cells also take nutrients needed by the body's other cells. Eventually the uncontrolled cells pile up and push into healthy tissue. Cancer cells can cause so much harm that the organism dies.

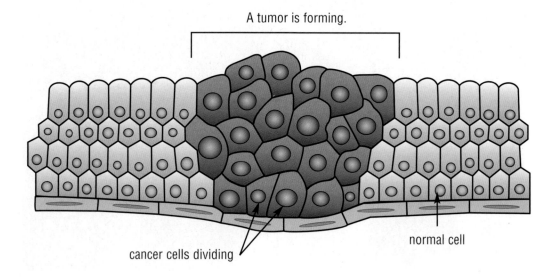

A tumor is forming.

cancer cells dividing

normal cell

Wrong Instructions

Sometimes there are mistakes in an organism's genetic information. As a result, certain cells get the wrong instructions. Parents often pass on genetic mistakes to their offspring.

Sickle Cell Anemia is a hereditary disease that affects many African Americans. One in 600 gets the disease by inheriting a flawed gene from both parents.

One genetic mistake in humans causes red blood cells to form incorrectly. Instead of their normal disk-shape, the cells look like hooks. But this hook, or sickle, shape prevents the cells from doing their job properly. As a result, they die quickly. Without enough red blood cells, a person gets sick. This disease, called sickle cell anemia, can lead to death.

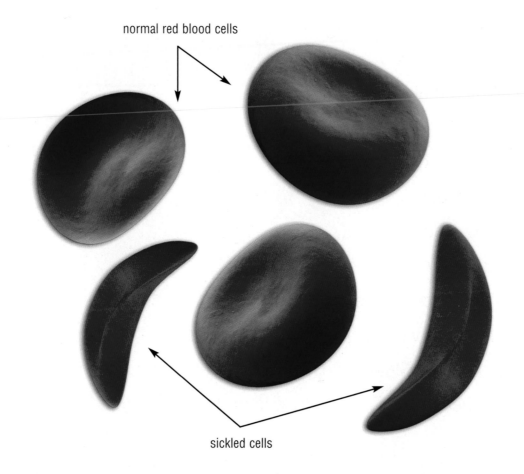

normal red blood cells

sickled cells

Traveling Genes

Cells can also malfunction when under attack. The tiniest attackers are **viruses**. A virus, made of just a few chemicals, is like a little traveling packet of genetic instructions.

A virus is not alive on its own. But it seeks to make copies of itself. In order to do that, it must invade a cell. When it does, the virus takes control. It forces the cell to make more viruses. After a cell produces many viruses, it often bursts. Meanwhile, the newly-created viruses invade other healthy cells. The process goes on and on.

DID YOU KNOW?

Many different viruses attack humans. They include measles, mumps, and chickenpox. Viruses cause colds and flu, too. AIDS is also a virus.

How a Virus Invades a Cell

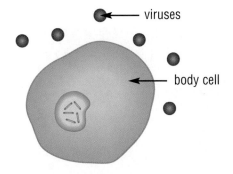
viruses

body cell

1. Virus enters cell.

Scientists have identified about 5,000 viruses. Some attack plant cells and bacteria, too.

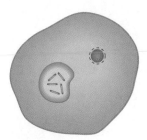

2. Substances in the cell begin to strip off the virus's outer coat of protein.

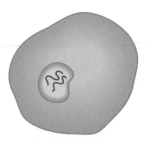

3. The nucleic acid in the center of the virus is released into the cell's chemical manufacturing system.

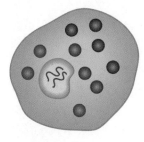

4. The cell ignores its own chemical needs and switches to making the virus.

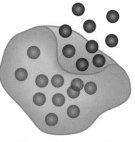

5. The cell is sometimes destroyed in the process. Many of the new viruses are released to infect other cells.

Single-celled Invaders

Bacteria are everywhere. Most are harmless, but some cause disease. Once inside an organism, these harmful bacteria start dividing quickly. They also take nutrients meant for the organism's cells. Certain types of bacteria even produce poisons, called **toxins**. These toxins can kill healthy cells.

Some bacteria live permanently in our intestines. They help us to digest our food.

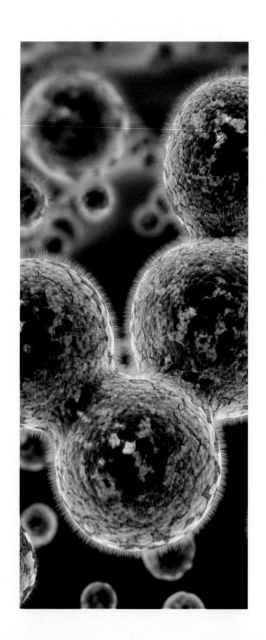

Bacteria Overload

In humans, bacteria are the cause of many ailments. These fast-producing invaders can cause ear infections and strep throat. Toxins from certain bacteria can cause a type of food poisoning called **botulism**. Bacteria also cause disease in other animals and plants.

Salmonella bacteria can grow easily in many foods. To prevent illness, people should prepare and store food safely.

CHAPTER FIVE

Science and the Cell

In the 1830's, German scientists Mathias Schleiden and Theodor Schwann called cells the basic unit of life. Since that time, scientists have learned a great deal about the cell. Gregor Mendel's experiments with garden peas in the mid-1800's showed that genes were the basis of heredity. A hundred years later, other scientists were studying DNA's structure and chemical make-up.

Theodor Schwann is also known for discovering a type of cell in the nervous system.

More Progress

By the late 1990's, scientists knew how to take genes from one organism and put them into another. Some doctors began to use the technique, called gene therapy, to treat certain human diseases. Their success was limited, though.

James D. Watson, shown here, worked with Francis Crick to discover DNA's unique, twisted ladder structure in 1953.

Into the Future

Today, scientists have mapped nearly all the genetic instructions found in human cells. This information has helped researchers locate the sources of many cell diseases. Scientists also are learning more about stem cells. These unique body cells are able to produce many other types of cells.

Parent and Child Identical

Some scientists have even learned how to produce an organism with the same genetic material as one parent. Researchers have used this technique, called **cloning**, to make some plants and animals.

Scientists use many tools to perform genetic experiments. Microscopes help scientists see changes in cells. Forceps are used to place a small piece of leaf in a microfuge tube.

Many Questions

New scientific discoveries can improve our lives. But we must think about the risks connected with this knowledge. For instance, gene therapy has many benefits. But should parents use this technique to change their future child's traits? Also, should scientists ever have the right to clone humans?

People throughout our society have different opinions about these issues. What do you think?

The next generation of scientists will learn even more about the cell and its workings.

GLOSSARY

antibodies (AN-ti-bod-ees): weapons produced by white blood cells to fight disease

bacteria (bak-TIHR-ee-uh): common single-celled organisms that sometimes harm humans

botulism (BACH-eh-lizm): a type of poisoning caused by a bacteria's toxin

cells (selz): basic units of life

chlorophyll (KLOR-uh-fil): green matter inside chloroplasts that absorb the Sun's rays

chromosomes (KROH-muh-sohms): threadlike structures in the cell that carries genes

cloning (KLON-eeng): making an organism with the same genetic material as one parent

fertilization (fur-tuh-li-ZA-shun): uniting the male's sex cell, or sperm, with the female's egg

genes (jeens): units in chromosomes that contain instructions passed from parent to offspring

meiosis (my-O-sis): the process in which a parent cell divides twice to produce four sex cells, each with half the chromosomes of the parent

mitosis (my-TOH-sis): the process in which a parent cell divides one time, making two exact copies of itself

neurons (NOOR-ons): nerve cells

nucleus (NOO-klee-uhss): the control center for the cell, which contains the chromosomes

photosynthesis (foh-toh-SIN-thuh-siss): the process by which green plants use the Sun's energy to turn carbon dioxide and water into food, giving off oxygen as a by-product

pollinate (POHL-I-nate): to transfer pollen to a flower's pistil

toxins (TOX-ins): poisons produced by organisms such as bacteria

traits (TRATES): qualities that make one organism different from another

vacuole (VAC-u-ole): a large sac for fluid inside a plant cell

viruses (VYE-ruhss-es): tiny chemical packets containing genes that invade living cells in order to reproduce

Index

Websites to Visit

www.cellsalive.com

www.bam.gov/sub_diseases/index.html

www.exploratorium.edu/traits/cell_explorer.html

About the Author

Susan Markowitz Meredith likes to learn about the nature of things. She especially enjoys sharing what she discovers with young readers. So far, she has written 40 books on a variety of topics, including natural science. Ms. Meredith also has produced quite a few TV shows for young thinkers.